A ROOM IN
California

Also by Laurence Goldstein

A ROOM IN *California*

Laurence Goldstein

TriQuarterly Books
Northwestern University Press
Evanston, Illinois

TriQuarterly Books
Northwestern University Press
Evanston, Illinois 60208-4170

Copyright © 2005 by Laurence Goldstein. Published 2005 by TriQuarterly
Books/Northwestern University Press. All rights reserved.

Printed in the United States of America

10 9 8 7 6 5 4 3 2 1

ISBN 0-8101-5161-8 (cloth)
ISBN 0-8101-5159-6 (paper)

Page 10: Photograph courtesy of the author

Page 36: Randolph Rogers (American, 1825–92), *Nydia, the Blind Flower Girl of Pompeii,* 1861, carved marble; gift of the Rogers Art Association (1862.1); courtesy of the University of Michigan Museum of Art

Library of Congress Cataloging-in-Publication Data

Goldstein, Laurence, 1943–
    A room in California / Laurence Goldstein.
      p. cm.
    ISBN 0-8101-5159-6 (pbk. : alk. paper)—ISBN 0-8101-5161-8 (cloth :
alk. paper)
    I. Title.
    PS3557.O396R66 2005
    811'.54—dc22

2004025482

♾ The paper used in this publication meets the minimum requirements of the American National Standard for Information Sciences—Permanence of Paper for Printed Library Materials, ANSI Z39.48-1992.

for NANCY

CONTENTS

ACKNOWLEDGMENTS

My thanks to the editors of the following magazines, in which these poems first appeared: *Boulevard* ("On Rereading 'Ode to Duty' "); *Connecticut Review* ("August"); *The Formalist* ("Languor," "Rock Star"); *Good Foot* ("What to Put on Walls"); *Iowa Review* ("Firmament on High," "Isaac and Mae," "Meeting the Graiae," "Millennium's End," "To Radcliffe Squires"); *Margie* ("Consummation"); *Michigan Quarterly Review* ("A Room in California, 1954"); *Mississippi Review* ("Lerner Meets Bella Darvi"); *Ontario Review* ("Dragon Lady," "Eutopia," "Scrapbooks," "Who Am I?"); *Poetry* ("*English Drawings and Watercolors, 1550–1850*," "Posies," "War Babies, Sixty Years On"); *Salmagundi* ("The Celebrity"); *Southeast Review* ("Paris in the Twenties"); *Southwest Review* ("Epistle to a Longtime Friend"); *TriQuarterly* ("Meetings with Prester John," "Through a Glass Darkly, 1998," "Untimeliness"); *War, Literature, and the Arts* ("The Harlot Robed in War"); *Washington Square* ("Old Mortality").

"Randolph Rogers: *Nydia, the Blind Flower Girl of Pompeii*" appeared in *A Visit to the Gallery*, edited by Richard Tillinghast (Ann Arbor: University of Michigan Museum of Art, 1997).

"Meeting the Graiae" was reprinted in *The Year's Best Fantasy and Horror*, edited by Ellen Datlow and Terri Windling (New York: St. Martin's Press, 2001).

"A Room in California, 1954" was reprinted in *Secret Spaces of Childhood*, edited by Elizabeth Goodenough (Ann Arbor: University of Michigan Press, 2003).

"The Celebrity" was reprinted in *Jewish in America*, edited by Sara Blair and Jonathan Freedman (Ann Arbor: University of Michigan Press, 2004).

A ROOM IN
California

One

So obvious who you weren't and would never be:
some swaggering giant-killer named Duke
who bulked in your fantasy life big as a derrick.
His trading card became your specialty:
you paid three Warren Spahns for one Duke,
you improvidently swapped Mantle for Snider,
lords of center field, worthy of worship.
You cut out his pictures from *Sport* and put them in scrapbooks.

Scrapbooks became more interesting than cards.
So many people were not-you, living and dead:
murdered Bobby Greenlease, your own age and build;
men who waved swords, rode horses, hewed rafts;
movie stars in nearby Hollywood and Bel Air,
even one nicknamed Duke, most goyish of all;
feature-length obituaries, those spots of irreversible
time; and, furtively, photos of female pulchritude.

Whatever welcomed, and prolonged, the gaze
got glued onto the oversize pages, crazy collage,
more objects than a museum room's occult keep.
Favorites were the sea's profoundly hidden forms:
sea fans and sea whips, fairy bass, horny corals,
and all mixed identities—the deadly lionfish,
squirrelfish, goatfish, and, most suggestive, angelfish.
Abyssal creatures never to be witnessed in real life.

Piled one after another in the cedar chest
emptied of bridal garments, now a wonderland
nightly accessible: the jungles of Honduras,
Celtic monasteries, all Seven Wonders
(only the Colossus of Rhodes figured in dreams).
You pored over anywhere-but-here, pasted in
semiotica of the future when you would pilgrimage
to outer copies of your inner pictureland.

Scrapbooks omitted only you, their maker,
who passed through their pages, a phantom
filling hours by sharing their truncated lives.
A school of one's own, a domain of one's own
for timely, two-dimensional reverie.
No friend intervened in your solitary subspace,
those fractal networks, those secondhand
harvests of what seemed the Higher Mysteries.

Holy scripture forbade you to make a world
abundant as God's, but this selective, eccentric
antechamber to the house of life you cherished
till childhood emptied in due course, and all toys
and talismans, all imperfect replicas and simulacra,
found their sanitary way first to recesses of the garage
and then in afteryears, while you studied in Providence,
to unrescued degradation in Time's trash heaps.

Dear scrapbooks, they have only this poem as tombstone,
a memorial for secret wonder, words for pictures.
When I open my gone anthology, what glows
in the well of memory, as ever, are the mirrors
made to distinguish the mature self, scholar
and fisher king, from the ocean-of-all-there-is:
serpent starfish extending long flexible arms;
cunning jewfish in its deep crevice, waiting for prey.

To tell this story I have to start close-up:
the odor of schmaltz, the acrid tang of herring,
the obscene tint of gefilte fish—some affect
of tribal communion in the City of Angels.

Then add backstory: the day's gut-wrenching
last-minute win by the Rams, Bob Waterfield's
slow dance in the pocket—pump once, twice—and
a mile-long pass to Elroy "Crazylegs" Hirsch.

After the touchdown, the celebratory
late-afternoon ethnic feast, downtown,
"and then we'll pay a call on Aunt Esther,
poor woman, the last Jew in Boyle Heights."

So far this is standard-issue urban memory,
spot of postwar time for the nine-year-old
relishing the soon-to-be-served wonder of it all,
like Wordsworth's boy at the lakeshore waiting

for hooted echoes from the ghostly woods.
Spreading sour cream on my latkes,
savoring the *Yiddishkeit,* more pungent
than the plain English of West Side assimilation.

Here's what makes this story different, deep.
My father wraps my hand in his, leans,
whispers feelingly, "Look at that man behind you,
corner booth, in the gray suit and blue tie."

I catch the conspiratorial tone, drop
my napkin, bend down, fire a glance
at this simian heavy-browed object of more than
my scrutiny, none of which he acknowledges.

"That's Mickey Cohen," my mother hisses,
less awestruck and quick to add an epithet,
"the vicious gangster, he's killed plenty."
So I look again but never catch his eye.

Crazylegs was my favorite athlete; I piously
hoarded his cards, clipped his portraits from *Sport*,
lined up for his far-from-classic movie bio.
In reverie I still re-create his eccentric moves,

galloping down one sideline, Tom Fears
down another, and gathering the peanut-size
ball to his gold jersey with stupefying grace;
everyone in the stands would rise and shout him

into the end zone ten yards ahead of any tackler.
He was one kind of California idol,
faster and more nimble, a flash of spirit
wrapped in a body any boy would die for.

You see I'm being evasive. You know enough
about narrative to keep your eye on the cameo,
the significant fact sitting there in the deli
arching an eye at the eavesdropping staff

while his kreplach cools and thrilled
customers nudge spouses and kids like myself:
Look, they say, how brazenly crime's
famous agents live among us, nothing

like New York, but here too Murder Incorporated
has a franchise, a Jewish pantheon
to house the psychotics of our very own
chosen family, the FBI's most wanted

here on our prosperous frontier. They got Bugsy,
they'll get Mickey soon enough, so feast your eyes,
Larry, for some day you'll be sitting in a deli,
searching for some way to impress your friends,

and you'll say, "This place reminds me, I've got
a story of the '50s . . ." And we guarantee, as long
as you speak about this Prince of Israel, you'll be
the center of attention, the voice of your city.

THANKS FOR THE MEMORY

July 29, 2003

My oddest family keepsake? Sounds like
a workshop assignment, a parlor game,
a query from *Nostalgia* magazine.
But today of all days, I take out
this photo of Bob and Bing arm in arm
with my mother's sisters, circa 1947,
on some avenue in the Adams district of L.A.

Everyone in the family has a copy; my cousins
can join me in a chorus of the gilded tale:
how this glamorous twosome, on the road
to filming a *Road* movie, spotted the gaggle
of twentysomething girls in a photo shoot
on a front lawn, stopped the car, and,
manager in tow, asked if they could join in.

How could it happen? What did it mean?
That on a whim the nation's most familiar
voices and faces would mix their charisma
with ordinary folk and make a still
for generations of the Soltot clan to set on shelves,
to share with guests, to freeze a perfect moment
in the full sunshine of postwar California.

And how often I've heard my mother's plaint
that because I, a toddler, ran a fever
she wasn't a member of that happy few,

bantering long delectable minutes
with royalty from the silver screen. Mea culpa!
The fault is unredeemable, and five decades
have not lessened the sting, for her or me.

Today I take the photo from the drawer
and tell the sacred story, again, to my sons.
"It would be as if . . . ," but there's no comparison;
no stars will fall into their life on a summer day,
no like mementos will pass to their grandchildren.
That's the point! You were unique, Bob,
you were family, our centenarian, our lost youth.

Let's say

I spent my boyhood in the Rhineland,
one of the blond *Wandervögel,* drifting downriver
past the Lorelei, under the steep towers of Cologne,
outwardly a pagan, muscular, Aryan,
inwardly a partisan for the Spartakus-Jugend,
spying for my father's trade union cell in Mainz.
Prisoner of the Death Head Guard, he smuggled
from Gestapo headquarters coded messages:
      THE QUIET SHALLOWS YEARN FOR THE SHARK
      EVIL TURNS ITS OPPOSITE TO ITSELF
After he tunneled under a wall, we strangled a guard,
torched a munitions factory, laid plans
to stalk the beast to Berchtesgaden, and
with a carbine and silver bullet turn the Third Reich into

what? Some languid inversion near the Pacific,
way down the western coast, ur-Hispanic,
sun burnished, retrospective, live and let live;
some sleepy spot like the allergy-inducing
only used bookstore in Culver City, Stanley Brile's,
my summer asylum and backstreet agora,
more overflowing of fantasy, more steeped in dreams
than the canon of studio films set anywhere but there:
Mogambo Stalag 17 Shane The Robe Ivanhoe Moulin Rouge.

In the closetlike sweatbox behind the children's books,
beside the true crime and girlie mags, every *Life* lay in wait.

I put down my lemonade, turn on the news from Kosovo,
and leaf through one survivor: September 18, 1944.
"Let's all back the attack," says Cadillac,
"victory is our business." Farnsworth engineers
promise, "Eventually, after the war, you'll have
home television . . . in cabinets of your choice."
GIs march down the Champs-Élysées. Joseph Auslander
pens a "new *Iliad*" below classic photos of the Normandy boats:
    "When Homer called the roll and read the names
    Of the tall heroes plumed for war's wild courses,
    Their splendid spears a forest of bright flames,
    The frantic trumpets and the frenzied horses,—
    He sang his litany of names and places,
    Even as I, who am no Homer, sing
    Our lads, with light of battle in their faces,
    Who stormed a deadlier Troy one night in spring."
A glorious birthright for war babies like myself, a diction
one hungered to deserve, a nourishing speech of the gods

but let's say

I chose to stand my ground at Mons, a *tall hero,*
tall for my age, following my gun-toting dad as he led
the American armored division to the Nazi flank;
"A death trap," he chuckled. "Watch the infantry
close its iron jaws." I reveled in the great game;
I manned a machine gun. I took prisoners.
I was worthy of Homer's and Auslander's praise.

I looked up "simile":
"Hektor came on against them, as a murderous lion on cattle."
I looked up "pentameter":
"Who stormed a deadlier Troy one night in spring."

I watch my son watch the refugees in Kosovo.
They are war's real thing, not chess pieces, not lambs,
simply what shuffles ingloriously because it must.
The Unknowable. The stuff of next week's *Life*.
And when he returns to cyberspace, the reborn site
of Stanley Brile's vanished emporium, I shut off the screen
and open the memory stored on shelves, back issues
of occult childhood: June 19, 1944, July 2, 1945 . . .

Realms pressed together, glossy, akinetic.
Debutante balls at the Hunt Club; wildcat strikes at Ford;
backyard cooking; Swedish glass; lithium;
Dumbarton Oaks and Trader Vic's; Fala; four seasons
on a Nebraska farm; the all-American art of Grant Wood;
We Want Willkie; magic acts; Hollywood pinups—
I was the heir of all culture; I bought and brought home
bound pictographs from that airless cave, the past.
All the visuals of *Life* All the reportage
The splendid spears The frantic trumpets
The habit of saying to myself,

Let's say

Tactics dancing in his head, the son poles his craft
under the guns of Düsseldorf, biding his time
as he spells out mile by mile his self-definition:

archivist, scribe, witness, antitype of psalmist and bard.
The river is broad and swift, flows near squatters' houses,
in which the fate of nations is plotted by restless kids,
Kommandants of the twentieth century's happier half,
in free verse, free as the prose of personal histories
shelved alphabetically, renewable till death:
Not So Wild a Dream   Only the Stars Are Neutral   Out of the Night

ISAAC AND MAE

[*Los Angeles, 1955.*]

HE: You are perfect in all ways but one.
      A model Jewish wife, sweet natured, modest—
      when have you ever preened in a mirror?
      And how the children *kvell* from you!
      All six have your delicate good looks—
      all right, mine too, my deep-set olive eyes
      you love to stare into as if transfixed.

SHE: How am I imperfect? Tell me.

HE: Darling, yesterday you forgot again—
      you *always* forget—the *Yahrzeit* candle.
      Mother died two years ago today, blessing you
      who made her last home a heaven. Her word.
      "Isaac," she would say, "Mae is heaven sent,
      she brings the gift of life wherever she goes."

SHE: I loved your mother too. How she cooked!
      And made the kids choke down all that grease—
      chicken fat, chopped liver. Poor things!
      I never liked it either. Nor did you!
      We're happier now I rule the kitchen, aren't we?
      I have hundreds of recipes, and the whole
      Imperial Valley to furnish me peaches,
      lemons, grapes, those purple plums you favor,
      and the tart Granny Smiths from up north

I bake into pies, strudel, sauce for your latkes—
look, your mouth is watering like before a meal!
Your mother didn't always love me. On the crossing
she cursed me for a Delilah: "Keep away from my son,
shiksa!" "Go somewhere else on the boat! Go!"
My vows of conversion changed her mind.

HE: More than that, Mae. You charmed her
with German lullabies and that eerie ballad
of the storm on Venusberg. Charmed me too.
Jews are not deaf to the sorcery of love
though instructed in the cost of it, so *often*
and *wrongly* instructed, as you proved, didn't you?
You melted her heart. I was all she had left.

SHE: At the border she wanted to name me Ruth.
I said no, I would be named for the month.
We started new lives in famous Hollywood,
raising my first babies while you went back
into the Black Forest, this time with a gun.

HE: Do you remember that actress from *Lost Horizon?*
After the war she stopped you in our deli and said,
"Are these your four children? You look like a girl."
Our wayward life has been like a movie, nothing
romantisch, me selling dead meats on credit,
but think how many in our family had it worse.
Often I dream of my sisters, how the Nazis . . .

SHE: Let's forget the past. This is America.

HE: And you never put out the candle for Papa.
Don't turn away—I'm trying to be helpful.
I mark the day on the calendar. Listen,
this is a small matter. Let's not quarrel.

SHE: I didn't know your father.

HE: Such a gentle man . . .

SHE: Possum's birthday is next Sunday, remember.
She wants a day at the beach, a picnic.
I told her she could invite six. "Oh, Mom,"
she said, "three brothers and two sisters,
so I get *one* friend?" "Hush," I said,
"you're too fair for summer heat, too blond.
You'll burn. Not even oil will protect you."

HE: All day I've been thinking about my father.
I guess it's my *Hälfte des Lebens* this year,
the crossroads. How he wanted to survive.

SHE: Killed by the Nazis. I've heard the story.

HE: Nobody knows the story but me. I've lived
a lie. No, worse. I chose to forget the truth.
Why should it drum and drum at me all day?

SHE: I have things to do. Shopping. Skippy needs
a ride to skating practice—no, it's Tuesday—
he needs a ride to . . . Oh, it's on the calendar!
Go look!

HE: We fled from the Nazis, yes.
How it all comes back to me. Nineteen thirty-nine,
January. We got news of another sweep.
Papa and I set out for the *Schwarzwald*,
some refuge so dismal even the Nazis
would let us two helpless Jews alone.
A snowstorm like you could never imagine,

dearest, or none of our children, or anyone
in this temperate part of the New World.
Snow more deadly than bullets, our bones ice cold.
Lost, we staggered forward like golem.
We came to a river, and no way to cross.
No ferryman, but his hardwood hut
stood open for us to die in. We lay down . . .

SHE: I will honor your father. I will light the candle!

HE: . . . and we slept without hope of waking up.
Yet I did wake. The storm blew open the door
and a woman appeared. Don't stop me!
I haven't told this to anyone for half my life!
A snow maiden, pale as the blondest *Walküre*,
robed in white with a belt of twisted steel.
She glided to my father and breathed into his face
till he turned blue, then ghastly. Her swan's neck
swiveled and suddenly her face was bending down
to give me the kiss of death. I gazed into her eyes
and she into mine. She said, "You are too handsome
to kill, far too handsome. I will not end your life
now. But if you tell anybody, even your mother,
what you have seen this night, I shall return
and slay you." Was it a dream? At dawn
the ferryman came and hid me three weeks more.
Mother and I passed safely to Italy, and a boat
to America. You approached us on deck, as beautiful
as the apparition who gazed deep into my eyes. . . .

O God! O God of my fathers! The way you look. . . .
Mae, it turns my blood cold. Why
are you so angry?

SHE: It was I, I, I!
I told you I would kill you, *I*
breathed death into your Jewish father.
And I would take my revenge, except
for the children. Now you had better
take very good care of my motherless
Kinder. If they ever complain, I will come back—
I swear it with my eagle's heart!—and
turn you into nothing more than dust.

[*She fades into mist that flies through a window. He stands in the silence of the house, listening to the wind shriek once, then become calm.*]

> I predict that the world as we know it
> will cease to exist on August 18, 1999.
>
> *Criswell Predicts* (1968)

Criswell, you were my favorite TV personality, fifteen minutes of high-voltage prophecy daily on Los Angeles Channel 13.

"Pomp and Circumstance" announced your shadowed presence at a table, visibly straining at the last bars to start your rapid-fire reportage.

And then the spotlight, the camera dollying forward to catch the fervor of your mad eyes and throbbing baritone:

"I predict . . . that the strongest earthquake in the history of the U.S. will virtually wipe out the city of San Francisco on April 7, 1975. . . . I predict the destruction of Denver by some strange and terrible pressure from outer space. . . . I predict the assassination of Fidel Castro by a woman on August 9, 1970. . . . I predict the renaming of every male child in the Soviet Union to Joseph in honor of the late premier. . . ."

You were the authentic voice of paranoid America, rattling off details of the apocalypse like the ticker on Walter Winchell's desk.

(That desperate old relic unmasked by television as everyone's lunatic uncle, telegraphing anticommunist scoops to all the ships at sea.)

And then you would ask us, if we saw you on the street, to shake hands, embrace, "for that is the only way we can conquer our loneliness."

I knew your voice from Sunday school Bible readings at the Reform synagogue. Yes, I could imagine Jeremiah on television, shaking a shepherd's staff and threatening no rain till Hollywood stopped making movies like *The Seven Year Itch*.

And then you would show up at the Iowa picnic along with Vampira to plug your new half-hour format and remind the nomads of Bellflower and Tarzana that eighty-seven percent of your predictions came true.

(The number is not implausible; even if you claimed constantly, as you did, that the U.S. would soon introduce contraceptives into the water supply to achieve less than zero population growth, you could cover yourself by intoning, after the show, "The sun will come up in the east. And set in the west. And then come up in the east. . . .")

Criswell, I confess that you scared me with your sibylline prevision of the warlord you named the Prince of Darkness rising from the Asian steppes in 1976 to overwhelm the world—you hinted that he might land his hordes on Sunset Beach and herd my family into slave-labor camps.

The hydrogen bomb and your program made a perfect fit—one signified that the end of days might be next week, and the other was a covert message of hope:

The world would endure a few more decades, at least, until the runaway planet you called Bullarion annihilated great cities and caused every volcano to "wreak fiery havoc" for many years.

(There was a bonus: Atlantis would finally pop to the surface, as Edgar Cayce too had foretold.)

How eerie it was to walk in the doomed terrain of Culver City after your dinnertime broadcast,

Down the reeking mudflats of La Ballona Creek, past the Toddle House, where realtors arranging the sell-off of Baldwin Hills could seal their deals and ogle some ladies of the night.

Hardly Babylon, I said to myself, spying some tired hooker and her john trudge two doors down Washington Boulevard to a cut-rate motel.

What did it matter which sins were performed or repressed? Enough to breathe in the pre-smog Pacific breezes, tinged with oleander and eucalyptus,

Enough to dance on the eve of destruction to rock 'n' roll denounced by city fathers as the devil's music channeled through the throats of Little Richard, Eddie Cochran, and the Ronettes.

Criswell, I miss your ravings about UFOs and truth serums and anti-gravity devices. Now it takes twenty stations to purvey the nonsense you distilled into a quarter hour.

Your brevity left me plenty of leisure to sit down with Poe and Lovecraft, and later with Yeats and Blake, and find their orphic prognostications not so different from your own.

So—thank you for inoculating me as a youth fated to live through the last decade of the second millennium after the amazing birth prophesied by Daniel and Isaiah.

The sun came up today in the east, just like you would have predicted, and when I think of August 18, 1999, I don't panic;

Thirteen percent of the time you were wrong, including the day of your own death, scarcely noted even on Channel 13. And what about the fateful night of March 10, 1990,

When, according to you, citizens of Mars, Venus, Neptune, and the moon would meet in Las Vegas to chart the future of the cosmos and try their luck at the slots?

I'm placing *my* bet that on August 19, 1999, a few relieved stargazers like myself will lift a tall glass to you, Criswell, dreaming boy with no proper name on the banks of the Wabash, oracle of the infant electronic hearth, Nostradamus wannabe who made us war babies gasp in wonder and watch the headlines ever more keenly.

Perhaps you're walking the cloudy boulevards right now, with total prescience about the uncalendared eternity to come;

It's not heaven exactly, more like the microwave ether of a billion billion transmitted signals, a place of no unmediated word or person, Videoland;

Airtime erased in living rooms is perpetually present in this dreamspace, including you, Criswell, in your Liberace suit of purest white silk,

And who would have predicted how many fans are flocking to you on their angel wings and dancing around your beaming spirit like happy geese in a halo of light?

DRAGON LADY

Fading, my pagan-summer-in-Catalina-
Island's umber complexion, the deep kiss
on skin of so much glad day, whitening
like the pages of Faulkner and Yeats I scrutinized,
sophomore grind further from Avalon than twenty-six miles.
November 2, 1963,
I was driving on Wilshire Boulevard, admiring
not only the chic new shops in Beverly Hills,
the Jaguar dealership, the bistros with French names,
but my twenty-year-old face in the rearview mirror.

I'm guessing that the radio played the year's hit song,
"Those Lazy-Hazy-Crazy Days of Summer,"
already nostalgic for the romance of August,
not the preacher's dream of being free at last
but chaste horseplay with cabin boys, fellow
proletariat at an overpriced hotel,
sweaty scrimmages, water jousts, wrestling
Bobby Levin's younger body into taunting surrender.
Lawrence of Catalina, Bobby called me, after
the year's big movie, while we sunbathed near White Cove.

The music stopped. And then a bulletin
not many Top 40 listeners would heed:
A coup in Vietnam. Diem dead. Nhu dead.
Madame Nhu would hold a press conference,
very soon, in the Beverly Wilshire Hotel.

I bluffed my way into the VIP room,
exotic as some cold war outpost
or posh screening room at the Directors Guild.
The fourth estate pointed cameras, joked
about the Dragon Lady, awaiting her mad speech.

Madame Nhu was famous for savage remarks.
First Lady of a foundering state, she loathed
the Buddhist monks who torched themselves:
"Let them burn," she said, "I will be glad
to supply the gasoline, and we shall clap our hands."
Named Le Xuan, Beautiful Spring, she spoke
no Vietnamese, only that French patois
shared by the colonized upper class.
Beautiful and cruel, more Lilith than Eve,
she doubled as serpent in the Orientalist press.

She was beyond my comprehension, I with
no insight into politics, no experience of grief.
She entered the room, close to me, so close
I could touch the color of moonlight she wore.
She said, "Now President Kennedy
has all the power he wants. But will he
be able to *hold* power? Power will be
dangerous for him too, more than he knows."
So few people there, why should she not
stare at me, so much younger than the rest?

Her gaze eclipsed the light of August, her voice
dubbed over Bobby's blithe chatter
pricking the mind like Catalina warbler cries
and our teasing farewells after Labor Day.
"I can predict to you," she fixed *me*
in the front row, "that the story of Vietnam

is only at its beginning." And so the fifties ended,
though none of us note takers wrote this down.
None saw how this stock femme fatale
spun out the sixties' thread before our eyes.

She donned her dark glasses, left the hotel;
I lingered, stunned, in the afterglow of glamour,
musing on her fierce incitement to war.
She departed the short memory of the West
except one day, three weeks later, when she
stepped from her Roman villa, now in black,
and spoke no sympathy for Jacqueline,
her Catholic twin. The days got shorter.
Los Angeles knows nothing of winter's
harrowing; still, nothing was ever the same.

Innocence, wrote Graham Greene, in his novel
of Vietnam, should wear a bell, like a leper,
to warn of its approach. Do I agree?
Surely, America had earned a respite, a time
for blamelessness, a right to say no
when Madame Nhu conscripted not just ourselves
to spread fire in her land. "I believe," she said,
"that all the devils of hell are against us."
Too innocent to resist, too arrogant in our
postwar fortune, we devils signed her pact in blood.

Put the blame on Mame. Call her Medusa,
this bit player, this contra-leper who vanished
ten years before the fall of Saigon.
Call her the evil muse of anticommunism, visiting
in spirit two presidents, their armies, all
who misconstrued her prophecy in Beverly Hills:
"What is done against Vietnam will be felt

in America, too." Felt in our politics,
I supposed she meant, felt as a wound to honor,
a stain from naively wooing the wrong side.

Trust TV to put on a happier face.
Look, our new partners in Hanoi sign a trade
agreement, a bonanza-to-be for ex-enemies.
Lawrence of Arabia is on cable, faded
in ideology and sienna tone of all that sand.
At the end, the uncrowned king travels home,
his wrinkled eyes stare bleakly down the road.
I know how he feels: history's ghost
free at last from the blissful dream of utopia,
watching the fatal motorcycle roar into view.

Then the cameras are somewhere else; they catch
liftoff toward Mars, psychic healing,
the lords of grunge rock, the khaki-clad
militiamen shaking guns in the public face.
In Washington last spring I touched the name
of Bobby Levin, trying to remember
thirty years of headlines we never shared
and how he looked in Avalon, milliseconds
before he stepped on a land mine near Pleiku.
You'll wish that summer could always be here

Two

POSIES

Flowers are a tiresome pastime.

William Carlos Williams

Who has written their language
more studiously than you, American poet?
Some as common as air,
some esoteric as the Zohar,
of a genus not visible on my planet.

No botanist, your standard
rose-and-tulip man, I
have gathered into my greenhouse,
under the skull, a glossary of names
and let them soak like lily pads
or like the chromatin of ideas
before a culture changes its mind.

Tiresome as second nature
often is, imaginary flowers
are the teeming Graces of loneliness,
lending their abstraction
to the bliss of mornings, even in spring,
when the real shuts up its petals
or heat-stricken does a dying swan,
perfectly useless except to the soil.

UNTIMELINESS

after Arthur Miller

They sauntered at shoreline, where the breakers fell,
pensive husband and glamorous wife.
Today, Sartre had it right: hell
was other people who preyed on their life.

Distant objects relieved the eye:
four fishing boats by the peach-
colored horizon, gulls in the sky,
and, suddenly, trucks on the beach.

A turning winch raised a net
bulging with fish, the sea's produce,
and dumped for transport the ill-fated
thrashing creatures, a silvery sluice

of never-ending energy, flowing west
into the insatiable guts of mankind.
"They know they're caught," she gasped, in her best
movie voice, and he, resigned,

steered her from what was more heartless,
the workers heaving aside inedible
sea robins, their corpses-to-be an artless
mosaic on the strand: waste as incredible

to tender souls as extinction of species
or triage in the traffic and brute neglect
of displaced persons, gypsies, refugees—
fish out of water fishermen reject.

"Why don't you put them back?" she said.
"Would they live again if they had water?"
Bending her beautiful body, she laid
fingertips on the day's slaughter—

too slippery! He intervened, a hero
flipping junk fish to the waves,
one by one, back to a perfect zero.
He emptied all their sandy graves.

"They'll live as long as they can," she laughed.
"That's right, they'll live to a ripe old age
and grow prosperous," he chaffed
her as they strutted merrily offstage,

he blessing her, hope in his eyes.
"Oh, how I love you," she said.
Thinking, For the moment nothing dies,
nothing on this shoal of time is dead.

RANDOLPH ROGERS: *NYDIA, THE BLIND FLOWER GIRL OF POMPEII*

The big doors close out what's contemporary:
the noise of a living culture, the earthshake
of lurid bulletins, each a brutal crime.
Always I glide first to this arresting figure,
the wrought shape of Bulwer-Lytton's fancy,
Nydia, flower girl in the last days of Pompeii.

Paired with a statue of Flora, she signifies
the frailty of cities, their last extremity
when Nature throws down its ruinous fire.
Not daisies but a broken capital at her feet.
She reminds the museumgoer how to look
at Death and Judgment waiting in the wings.

Hell is underneath her, and a heaven of ash
falls on the stampeding pagans swirling around.
She hears their shrill scream, "The hour has come!"
Tense with angelic purpose, she cups her ear
for the unchoked response of one beloved voice.
"Take my hand, Glaucus, thou shalt be saved!"

Streetwise, lowborn, never to be romanced
or idolized, Nydia must endure
a calamity worse than Vesuvius, his love
for a priestess of the Cross, a figure of light
luring him to the cultic vision of paradise.
The blind girl worships no deity, only him.

Nydia now is the very emblem of Psyche,
better off in the dark, bent downward,
carved in the posture of maidens pursued
by a fatal lust, or sacrificed, like Antigone
the staff of Oedipus, another casualty
of the classical gods who so hate mankind.

In museums catastrophe has a privileged place.
All who walk through this temple of art
suffer the need for some redemptive voice.
Can Whistler or Monet strike so deep?
More than landscape this witness of world's end
pulls one, spellbound, close, closer. . . .

Twenty-five years I have visited you.
Gazed at your sealed orbs and upward
where the imaginary smoke of extinction
gathers like the vanished clouds of 1945.
"Terror of Nature." And you her mute survivor,
untouchable, except in these marble lines.

TO RADCLIFFE SQUIRES

in memoriam

"The dangerous magic of human memory."
You envied that phrase by Frederic Prokosch,
and his pretty-boy looks, and his year of fame.
Shyly, you showed me a studio photo once,
yourself as his double, girl-glamorous,
prewar faun's flesh unwrinkled as Narcissus.
The Asiatics whispered to your generation:
journey among the wicked vanities
and turn what is "tarnished, perverse, epicene"
into vignettes the world will savor secondhand,
keepsakes for an afterlife of vanished esteem.
You hero-worshiped this vagrant who "had no master—
and hardly a peer," who never answered your letters
as you charted his intensities in an admiring book.

Prokosch abandoned verse; you took it up,
six postwar volumes of crystalline speech,
stanzas wind-carved as the Utah buttes.
Tracing these fey solitaries to their source,
I found a mercurial botanist, a connoisseur
gracing the house and garden with rare slips
from Olympus, cuttings from Andros and Carmel.
"Life is the only *pragma;* it is the only fact,"
you wrote in summarizing *The Skies of Europe,*
and neglect of your art did not entirely sour,
even in your seventies, the praise of life

you offered a few hundred readers till life
stopped one Valentine's Day and you put by
your spoiled body on that unnatural shore.

I wonder what made you love, so much and so long,
the maker of *The Carnival,* wayward, haunted,
the Shelley this century keeps from its schools.
The only unforgivable sin, you often said,
is to impersonate oneself. Of course,
but how many others are worth mimicking? One
model, at least, must drive the hungry spirit
among otherworldly gardens, the Asia of poets.
Love will crown the voice of a generation.
You never knew celebrity, not even a year,
but your obscure life grows somewhere still,
in human memory like mine, in the exotic herbs
you divided among friends, in the language
you made a dangerous magic of. *Requiescas*

WHO AM I?

Mister, you can see I need work.
I'm a preindustrial serf, unskilled
in robot tool and die, spiteful about
the way a punch press crushes a head,
a blade shears an arm, a leg is drilled.
You know what it's like putting a finger
into the clammy hole of a garbage disposal,
that's my squeamish feeling every day
I contemplate the sharp edges of our culture.

I'm pleased we're entering a postindustrial
phase; I have hard-won talents for this one:
a programmer's savvy, an eye for moving pictures,
a willingness to amuse the privileged class.
Sure, I'll stack boxes in your warehouse
but, fair warning, I won't be satisfied,
I'll seek advancement when the system
suffers downtime in the blackout of self-doubt.
Misfits can be model citizens, too.

Till the space age workers' paradise
welfares me or gives me more power,
I'll slander it with epigrammatic skill
and wait for the oil to run out. I mean, why
put my underclass shoulder to the flywheel?
Another wheel is driving the managers down,

their kibitzers up. The blade is sharper.
Mister, I've had centuries of practice
biding my time. Show me where to sign my name.

MEETING THE GRAIAE

for John Barth

Perseus speaks

. . . to press my case. Hermes had said,
"Use eloquence, then violence."
All three were swan shaped, ugly
as the spinster Gorgons they guarded,
passing their eye each to each
for quick peeks at the baffling world.
They looked easy to outwit, aunts
who trade anything for words of love.
I began with customary epithets:
"Sisters gray from your birth,
gray shadows of the elder world,
give me not your eye or tooth,
not these remnants you share
in the holy spirit of community,
give me your vital secret. Now.
I need the address of the Nymphs
who keep the winged sandals, the cap
of invisibility, and the bag in which . . .
some enemy's head will bide its time."

They seemed to know my type: the hero
who spares them a tiny portion
of his immortality; still they demurred
so I had to get rough, and I can.
I seized their one viscous eye

and threatened to stomp it, fling it
deep into the Tritonian lake, or eat it.
Eerie screams you can't imagine, and then
the information. I stuck the jelly
into the nearest crone's empty socket
and resumed my fabulous destiny.

You know the rest. I slew Medusa,
stabbed to death the sea fiend
who would have made Andromeda
its meal (she was delicious, then).
I should write my own epic deeds;
instead, past my lurid prime,
I ponder the meaning of it all.
The supreme stuff of Zeus is in me
yet I feel infirm as the Graiae,
as if I were part of *their* story,
a chance adventurer, bold
but nothing extraordinary,
nothing they couldn't serenely outlive.
On visits to great Olympus, I'm sure
those witches entertain the gods
with *my* story, the task-oriented hunk
unworthy of a wandering eye,
one of many interruptions of their
endlessly fascinating lives, a speck
of mortal time, like a gaudy sunset.
The gods have heard it all before,
so often they lip-synch every phrase—
no text is sacred to those know-it-alls.
Yet they applaud; the story's on *me*,
boy wonder, latest has-been. . . .

Yes, I do have other duties.
Send me a transcript of this interview.
I'll add it to my archive,
large enough almost for a room
in this inherited castle, grand,
richly appointed, though the kids
rarely visit, and never write.

Perfect for the quiet summer eve.
Nothing phlegmatic or provocative,
mainly mild admiration of the land,
cattle and cottages, horses, gypsies,
a sailboat launched on Windermere
like the soul in fair weather, upright,
unafraid of the crosshatch, likely a storm,
haunting the top left corner.

Turn the page, and keep turning.
Greyfriars Monastery, Rokeby Park,
St. Martin-in-the-Fields, archaic
as the blithe dreams of infancy.
Soothing and picturesque, each plate
muffles the noise of history, the rant
of tribal territorial claims:
art as refuge, stasis, silence.

But here's a gouache of different stripe.
A Young Daughter of the Picts wearing,
if that's the word, a tissue of tattoos,
nothing but the blazonry of roses and
vines blooming on her pale body.
Not entirely au naturel, she carries
a boar spear and a scimitar
hooked by a golden chain to her belt.

Forgive us, Wordsworth, if our eyes
linger on this barefoot girl
longer than on *View from Skiddaw*
or the green glades of Patterdale.
She too is a garden, seeming to invite
but warning, by her averted gaze,
she is off limits to the non-Pict,
a warrior no modern will cultivate.

What this daughter of time could yield
she entrusted to the artist, and he,
five centuries removed, to this book.
Her erotic force is unforgettable:
hand on hip, her fierce glamour
no less than her flower-shaped breasts
and the green overlay on her Venus mound
extend into tamer watercolors—

hummocks shimmering at sunset,
thatch roofs (with sheep) aglow.
One spark ignites the ensuing sheaves!
Now the poised out-of-doors incites
fresh respect for its visible hungers,
as if the world's body were susceptible,
always, to how we frame its energies,
how we suffer its beauties on our skin.

"For Heaven never hates the noble in the end,
It is for the nameless multitude that life is hard."

Euripides, *Helen*

Well spoken, Castor. You point the moral
and adorn, ex machina, the preposterous tale
rumored in Herodotus, that *la belle Hélène*
did not *really* set horns on Menelaus,
no, that was an airy double shaped by Hera,
who transported the actual daughter of Zeus
to Africa, there to wait out the matter of Troy.
How Menelaus, in beggar's rags, is reunited
with his Spartan bride, and Ulysses-like
outwits the Egyptian sovereign who covets her—
that is Euripides' fairy tale of the ruling class.
Has anyone ever taken this version seriously?
Even the author, in other plays, sees your sister plain
as Homer's vain adulteress, the beauty who laid
so many warriors low, the noblest in the end.

In the heaven of art, their fame is everlasting;
these royals resume their privilege, make love
in scented sheets, replicating their kind.
But you finish your speech, starry twin,
by rightful allusion to the underclass,
the ignoble, hoi polloi, the grunts
unnoticed by Homer, whose skulls were crushed
under chariot wheels and whose quick burial
was unaccompanied by festive games and gifts.
"You mean," asks Menelaus's worn-out servant,
"it was for a cloud, for nothing, we did all that work?"
Truest and most timely line in tragedy,

it deserves truth in response: Yes, *all for*
nothing that epic war, and all its victims
dead for no reason, for the ghost of a reason.

Of the many Troys for Helen to burn
the Greek and Latin bards foresaw every one.
Readers late as myself longed, once,
to join the fleet and win sinful favors
from the muse of battle; her Leda visage glowed
in the text, her figura followed us to bed.
In later years, whenever her beauty rose
upon our gaze in movie palaces,
brazen rationale for war against Reds or Blacks,
we made choral speech to the unversed:
Don't be fooled, don't pledge your self to her body,
she is no *real* incentive, no woman at all,
a goddess of light, fantasy's phantom bride,
piece of propaganda poured by executives of
Universal into the lowest cut of sky-blue gowns.

No moviegoer, no male gawker at Venus,
is a pacifist at heart; no feminist
either who suffers the compliment of power:
"Frail, yet you launch a thousand ships!"
Art checks us if we seek shelter in art:
wised up, having read the classics,
even the most thoroughly seduced of men
may rise as from unmarked plots and drift,
with the pardlike grace of an Atreus,
to high ground above Troy, purged
of bloodlust, loving the lowly infantry,
their spear-bitten limbs, their naked sex,
their hearts' tragic untutored obedience.
At the end of enchantment, double-tongued Castor,
lies something purer than the Muses' spring.

After the success of her film *The Egyptian,* the
actress lost the patronage of Darryl Zanuck and
ended her career as a prostitute on the Riviera.

B.: Back to the camera, I unfolded with leprous hand
My robe and said to Sinuhe, "I have only this
To exchange for your great skill." L.: I saw you stand
At the chemin de fer table, lean over, and kiss
That hog jowl when he won the throw. How much
For a piece of that? I wondered. B.: "I have only this,"
I said and lifted his fingers to my breast to touch
The excited flesh, but he would neither touch nor kiss.
L.: Never mind all that. I was in the movie too,
A boy worshiper of Pharaoh's god, and my prayer
Was one day possessing you. Will fifty dollars do?
B.: I am engaged, completing my scenario of despair.
L.: No dice? OK. Who *needs* you, for Christ's sake?
B.: No person. I have only this . . . to give, and take.

A year later AP biographied the purged
And self-damned falling star, who took
With oven gas the denouement urged
by Lerner at Nice and the Egyptian in his famous book.

Most derided and feared of all midlife poems,
written by Urizen, according to Blake,
spineless, timid, counterrevolutionary,
gospel of "repose that ever is the same,"
of "self-sacrifice" and the "humbler" grace
manifest in the strong embrace of what's routine;
this testament of a former free spirit summons
an "awful Power" unpatriotic as a tax on fun.

"Ode to Duty" lies in wait on the Natchez Trace,
a traffic light on the interstate, always red,
the boulder no boomer can quite squeeze around
while making the triumphal ascent up Mt. Whitney.
Is this text the firm support of "love" and "joy,"
as Wordsworth claimed, or the rude ambush
at Merry Mount, the chasm into which generations,
imperial, libertarian, plunge to premature decease?

How will Americans make peace with this poem?
Its patristic exaltation of the "lowly wise,"
the way it bullies us to settle for less,
to acknowledge as deity not the unruly wolf
but the obedient Lab, collared and trained;
On the Road no longer, we cozy up with *Main Street,*
buy more insurance, vote, fund-raise for the schools;
chafe, nonetheless, in our wild Emersonian souls.

Duplicity, dear friend, is my game today;
writing an *open* letter to you, keeper
of my secrets, my all-too-candid and
never-to-be-disclosed self-battery—
be forewarned, my tone will be elevated,
my face to the world more poised, or posed.
Unlike our habit of confession, I'll pretend
to no sins and wait for your disbelieving review.

"The truest poetry is the most feigning,"
asserts my impossibly perfect model, Wystan
of the Crossways, tutor to Lord Byron, prophet
of the noncommunist empire for good and ill,
minting new currency, making new genders.
The genuine rigs the system, as gamblers know;
they too dissemble, poker faced,
as nosy cameras watch them place their bets.

Postmodern I'm not. The world isn't Vegas
though "crapshoot" is our metaphor, isn't it?—
even for the steep chances at love, and friendship,
we humans hazard via long distance,
sending the root flavor of our dwindling lives
by some latest Pony Express; "friendship
is the image of eternity," John Lyly wrote,
"in which there is nothing movable, nothing mischievous."

E-mail is most feigning, lacking even a signature.
Are letters a performance? We've exchanged many,
full of insidious delight: you've sent rumors
and I've responded with anecdotes, or other way round;
you've observed the local fauna; I've traveled
all the way to Kathmandu and flown over Everest.
On safari I've spotted a leopard, and you've
had your trips, sometimes while sitting still.

Always, we've believed in letters, both
the professional and personal kinds; we've tallied
our modest honors, as if we were modest,
and vented our discouragement—too many times!—
when wounded by the nasty world. We've played the role
of each other's spoiled child, too smart
not to take reciprocal pins to our inflating egos.
The child is father to the man but also a child.

Figure it this way: letters of the postal kind
are the ice floes we hop across, nimbly,
each a melting platform, ductile as the seasons.
"We have no truck with nonchalance," you wrote.
"We are the partisans of chalance." Yes, I suppose
our bulletins of distress in time of war, and
our crows of triumph at new masterpieces
not our own, qualify us as engagé.

So we've been entertaining and sententious;
articulate and glib; we've put our wit to the wheel;
Great Pretenders across vast distances—
pretending that you're still around, Alphonse,
pretending that you're still around, Gaston—
and suddenly we're sixty and suspect, for the first
time since 1962, we may expire
before the global ruin finally flames out.

How to feign not being alarmed? Be soigné
is my verbal style while tendering, gingerly,
that bloody subject, that fate accompli, making it
an inescapable topic between us, as if
it were a new locale, an *affaire de coeur,*
a Prize, a rude bit of northern climate:
all those tropes our favorite authors use
to signify the truest poetry of experience.

Our favorite aesthetician says the "late style"
eschews the conflict of elements, clouds over
distinctions in favor of unions: shantih   shantih . . .
Let's not relax into the world without binaries,
if only because we two are really two, and
have enjoyed butting horns as much as
grazing on Parnassus, chewing over
the same leaves of grass, then tumbling into dispute.

Sure, on occasion we've both feigned a reverence
for union with the cosmos, when the mind shuts down
and, bubbles on Time's aye-babbling stream,
we unselve ourselves. Then we re-mind
each other: the mystical rush is you-know-what
and we have no time to kill before Time
kills our appetite for correspondence, our
we-hope-witty monthlies of profound good cheer.

America being so large, we will live apart
to the austere end, I suppose. I'm trying to find
some elegant Audenesque way of saying
I wish it were otherwise. I wish we were
face-to-face not intermittently, but
every day, like this vernal one, watching
lilac and honeysuckle astonish the world
and birdlife we point to, then make our high five.

Letters have no artful closure: one writes,
then breaks it off. Verse epistles *seem*
to require a rounding or climax, but in this case
let art imitate art. I cease for no reason
so that, later, I'll pick the thread off its snag
and keep weaving with you this garment,
this lifelong vesture of form-fitting fleece
we exchange for a while—our opus of hours and our shroud.

Three

LANGUOR

after Verlaine

I am the Empire at the end of decadence,
Watching the blond barbarians' merriment
As I compose this idle ornament
Of gilded lines where languorous sunbeams dance.

Weariness of soul shrouds my existence.
Out there, they say, battles are turbulent.
Oh if I could kindle, lazy and impotent,
If I could will myself to rouse just once!

And why not bloom a little before I die?
Everything is stale! (Pretty boy, I see you grin.)
Everything is stale! All spent! Let the sack begin!

Only this stupid poem to burn by and by,
Only a Cynic's handiwork, modeled today
As rest from ennui, an empty spirit's play.

MILLENNIUM'S END

> The beginning is like a god which as long
> as it dwells among men saves all things.
>
> Plato, *Laws*

I

A baby screams in the night.
The new father holds his breath
and thinks, To stop that cry
I would torch Alexandria's
word-hoard, every microchip.
History would recommence with one purpose,
the muting of *that scream.*

II

How often, the year of graduation,
I thought of my fellow Californian
Kerensky, in his Berkeley soviet,
the mordant reproof he would offer,
like the actor he wished to be and became:
"Mr. Goldstein, citizen of the new frontier,
in your valedictory speech, 'The Voice of the Future,'
I notice you say nothing of dispossession
or thwarted desire, nothing of
the malignity of intellectuals
nor of Red czars who fatten on
the bovine simplicity of the urban poor,
nothing of *peace, land,* and *bread.*"

III

A card fastened by pushpin into cork,
a phrase written on it: "third stream"
asterisked in the *New World Dictionary*
as *new word:* a music combining
jazz improvisation with classical,
mostly twelve-tone composition. Think of
artists plotting this marriage, this
new fact of evolution, one with
The Gossamer Albatross and the fiber-optic brain.

IV

Leaving Providence for a new position,
year 2 of the Nixon era, I bequeathed
to the Salvation Army for reassignment
the shirts into which I had sweated
my dissertation, pans that had overcooked
three hundred meals of Scotch ham and beans,
my sets of Bulwer-Lytton and Walter Scott,
my caved-in chair cushions, my
worn-out carpet remnants
rubbed bare by history's Top 40 ideas—
I assumed that in Ann Arbor,
commune lately under siege,
I would create truth and see justice done.

That September, Robert Hayden said,
"I took no part in the Black Action Movement.
I voiced my epithets in new poems
crafted like the eloquence of Keats
or my fluent models Auden and Rukeyser,

who make their own music, like the soul.
Don't talk to me about Uncle Tom!
Haven't I imagined Malcolm's quest
as oh-so-true to our American gospel,
'Strike through the mask'?"

V

A telegram arrives, "Mr. Kerensky,
now is the dawning of the age of Aquarius."
Expletives in Russian, and a bitter scowl.
Yes, he is an emblem of the *provisional*,
fifty years of interminable waiting.
"A great world cataclysm has run its course,
and we are on the threshold of an unknown era,"
he writes in 1965.
But who is *he*? To Eisenstein, a peacock;
"a Bonapartist," said Trotsky, "who lives
in the Winter Palace, who sleeps in
the bed of Russian emperors." To Lola Ridge,
"flower the storm spewed white and broken
out of its red path."

He cannot outlive another war.
Now his prolonged Acts of memory,
his contra-Lenin, is finished for all time;
he is one with the transfiguration
imagined in the closure of his holy book.

VI

Open ye the gates, that the righteous nation
which keepeth the truth may enter in.

Perestroika was a beginning.
Those who struck through the wall
made a beginning, a halo of sky.
Animals became visible again; the body
glowed when May Day lost its terror.
I traveled to Washington with my sons,
"new Moscow" some called it online,
but redeemed in spirit since 1967,
when I marched on its guns. "Guns
will govern the future; don't tread
on me," the militiaman ranted,
wanting the war back again,
not Armageddon, a provisional war
righting the balance of power.
Time is a tunnel, I told my sons,
or several tunnels; and intermittently
we drive into the light. "*You* say it's the light,
we say it's the tunnel. . . . Look around, Dad."
The House of the People coiled in darkness
visible even on the Fourth of July.
An implacable speaker twisted his mouth,
raised his arm over the multitude: "Comrades . . ."
Suddenly I was fifty, grayer,
less creaturely, less eager for miracles,
planning retirement in the new century.

VII

Imagine the year 2099.
The binaries lie in ruins;
a third stream, blue skinned
and unclothed, more fond of fruit
than of anything on four feet,

assembles in the vacant condos of
the former czars, where it reads
Russia and History's Turning Point.
Since we have the freedom to say so,
let's pretend that several extinct species
have survived; they regenerate
and become local gods, flying or crawling.
Anthems are made in odd cadences
the voice must be trained to utter.

The point of such pretense is this:
the babies are sleeping again,
peaceful as underground pools
bathing the roots of evergreens,
they live in the provisional heaven
of perfect animal satisfaction.

VIII

One fall morning, writing this poem
and gazing for recreation
at the yellowing pears on the tree,
winter savories whether
for squirrel or human gourmets,
I saw a cardinal in the ocher leaves
turning the black mask of his visage
back toward whatever home he had left;
shaking his red crest he let flow
a loud slurred whistle of speech.
"New neighbor"—I almost said "new spirit"—
"make my dwelling less comfortable,
a habitation not a prison,
an origin not a refuge;
open the gates of my desire."

We know you only by metaphors:
gourmet feast we essay in schools,
a bouillabaisse hot served
on coming of age; cubist pantheon,
nine expatriate busts askew,
overlaid with gold; our lost Garden
more fruitful than the sand
we stand upon, with cacti and toads.

Great-grandparents, your inheritance
empties our pockets, muggers
of talent, prodigal madcaps
sealing your decade with a crash.

Can it be as we fear?
Not even the century's turn
has eclipsed your towers?
In 2020 we'll be tendered
a restorative, some ratafia
just like at La Closerie, only
this one will bring a centennial boon:
no end of time to praise
your advent, half naked as before.

ROCK STAR

The future cannot be overpraised. You live
to remind us how radiantly it gleams.
In spite of losers who did not survive,

who fell under the steep odds, you thrive,
make millions on the public's dreams.
The future cannot be overpraised. You live

a gaudy lifestyle, swank, appetitive,
flaunting your good looks and luck to extremes
in spite of losers who did not survive.

Some flamed out after one swan dive
or got discarded from the Beatles or Supremes.
The future cannot be overpraised. You live

in the afterfrenzy of your obsessive drive
to stay number one. Your ruthless schemes
in spite of losers who did not survive.

Don't look back! Don't pity! Don't give
a moment's heed to your rivals' screams.
The future cannot be overpraised. You live
in spite of losers who did not survive.

AUGUST

The agenda was so long, barium heavy,
clamorous meetings for others' benefit,
rarely your own, but you wrote the reports,
honorably returned every call, to placate,
conspire, assist, reprimand, acquiesce,
and having reached the bottom of the box, you fled
to some desert spot to sweat out the ego,
swim laps for the sake of insensibility,
compelled yourself, when curiosity sank
its feral tooth, to regard only the grass
browning and crackling underfoot, until
the occupational fit passed, and, a thing
among things, a parched hero of the spirit,
you advanced, by way of retreat, back
to your ninth-month dwelling, where the trees
dump their holdings, winds blow out
from the equinox, hissing louder than currents
circulating heat in the freshly dusted office,
and obligations fall upon your head like rain.

The ghost town is like . . . a ghost town.
Death Valley. Tombstone. Dry Gulch.
Tumbleweed blows into the mine's open mouth.

It's a place one comes to on the road.
More seductive than some, more candid.
A place where progress, thankfully, stops.

Novelists like it as a metaphor.
When travelers linger here, then settle,
the narrative finds its resolute finale.

In movies the lone rider traverses it.
There's a fertile plateau just beyond,
teeming with rivers and fat cattle.

Someone rustles them or sets them free.
If they wander into this domain, they die.
Their bleached bones enhance the mise-en-scène.

Men who wanted gold drifted this way.
The sun was their big yellow strike,
the witness of whatever panned out.

Newspapers that never reach so far
sometimes print a name, a picture:
a shack, a donkey, a backdrop of scrub.

One Mojave hermit said, "The silence
is God's cold brew on a scorching day.
I make friends with the barren soil."

Stars, those decent citizens, keep the peace.
They're just deserts of gas, worth less
than an unfenced acre of prickly pear.

Night is the glorious closure,
the prospector's taste of pure time,
time as the end of wanting more.

The sun rises, begins another circuit of hours.
Like the blind god it isn't, it glows,
then undergoes its irresistible routine.

Once, we loved our sister satellite.
Desert Endymions hot to shoot off,
we fashioned Cadillacs of ascent
to touch her dry Sea of Serenity.

What we thought heroic wasn't.
Our old moon, Sagan said, is "boring,"
like police photos of gelid bodies
icepicked in the heart or neck.

Mars is a nastier myth but
more seductive for some latter-day
atom-energized *Voyager*
to lay by, the better to fly by

and finally, beyond Pluto, settle among
Eocene forms not yet imagined,
not humdrum, resourceful as rodents,
"intelligent life" we fondly call it,

meaning smart enough to welcome *us,*
their destiny, but smarter than us too,
having no need for cinemas, jails,
or moving vans to find out what they are.

CONSUMMATION

Soldier, I took your life

        because the land was given us

because my leader said

        the enemy must be erased

and swore by our holy book

        we've known nothing but loss

I would be blessed in heaven

        having been dispossessed on earth

I would be made whole

        having been severed in history

So I prepared for martyrdom

        I came to the crossroads

a human bomb in black hood

        clasping my rifle at the ready

and when you came near me

        a uniform thinking of love

hurled myself on yourself

        a fervent embrace, a destiny

    Soul I will not recognize as mine
    Soul I will not recognize as mine

WHAT TO PUT ON WALLS

You wouldn't want a jay in a cage
blurting, day and night, its blue protest.
You wouldn't want the discard of neighbors,
their dull LPs, their pill canisters,
or that flat tire placed in the garden
alongside the purple iris and white rose.
(Some might, to make a fashion statement.)

So what do you choose to furnish
the huge conspicuous surfaces of your cave?
Rule out what's merchandised as chic,
what's common property for the middle class:
bulls made sense at Lascaux, but bullfight posters,
Chicago Bulls memorabilia, O'Keeffe-style
cow skulls, or big-sky vistas of cattle drives . . .
too much a bull market for those images
and *so much else* that's overexposed, however glam.

Something singular and, say it, beautiful,
neither mass produced nor someone else's ego
crowding the psychic spaces sacred to yourself,
something of the uncanny world to detain the eye:
a local artist's landscape of a site not far away—
you glimpsed eternity there—or a lover's letter,
like any shard of the past endless in implication;
some new lyric, some gleeful niece on a tricycle;

or put up nothing, an amplitude of nothing,
ringed by wood trim and blanker than
a Fontainebleau-size mirror wrapped and boarded,
waiting for shipment to the master glazier in Bruges.

For this burst of song, this salsa ode,
muchas gracias, Chicana beauty,
thanks for the wake-up hymn
arousing me from senior reverie.

This patch of shore was my stomping ground
forty years before you set foot
where white boys faced off muchachos
on the volleyball sand court,

taunting and aping in two lingoes
while the score climbed to twenty-one,
then sharing tacos and kosher meats
and whistling at girls in the sun.

You're not singing "La Cucaracha"
or "Vaya con Dios," my eighth-grade
carols of good-neighbor cheer.
What *is* the content of your serenade?

I hear the word *playa* on repeat,
so I listen for *amor* and hear it.
More hip-hop than crooning aria,
but no less caressing to the spirit.

Who knows where those other words
steer the sentiment? Now you laugh
and half dance to your own beat,
lost for a spell in self-choreograph.

Muse who sets me musing,
your pelvic thrusts and snapping hair
(long, full, and pitch black)
distract me from your gnomic patter.

A scholar, I *don't* think of Tula,
the Toltec capital, or Tenochtitlán.
I don't think of Malinche, the concubine
of Cortés, much less of Venus or Helen.

For once, I'm not in history,
not in time, only in lyric space,
listening, like a bird or angel,
to your wild cries of antic grace.

Senorita, I hear you rhyme
the infinitive for hearing, *escuchar,*
with . . . something I can't catch,
comunicar . . . flirtear . . . sonar?

I can't linger. Already your friends
have spotted me, paused at the wall.
As I stroll north, your joyful melody
fades into the music of the carousel,

the cries of preteens in bumper cars,
grunts of bodybuilders, sighs
of brown and white grandmothers
riding bikes for exercise.

At the boundary break of Ocean
I unlock my Voyager, settle down,
my fingers poised on the radio dial.
What *canción* are you singing, now?

OLD MORTALITY

Shriveled pear tree, hived with bees,
heavy with hard fruit I bite
to remind myself
Nature's often indigestible,

often bitter, often bland,

you shrink in the killing shade
of the flourishing walnut,
our neighbor's sole, untouchable success,
and lean so menacingly
toward our kitchen, our consummate joy

remodeled at a sultan's ransom
(my parents would say), adorned
with porcelain figures of my birth decade:
Josephine Baker, Claudette Colbert.

Bees nosh on your small, fallen pears,
sun granules, light scavengers;
where will they go when our fear
of what declines, however green,
uproots you, centenarian, and clears
the bay window of your familiar pose?

The past is not even past,
it occupies our living room,
the late century's whole
cosmopolitan collectible
ensemble of artifacts, not yet
archaic or quaint, though slipping
into, let's say, a *period* character,
some destined for museums,
some still the provenance
of *bricoleurs* like yours truly
and yourself, blue-eyed wife
who selected the love-struck author
fresh from his graduate clinch with Wordsworth,
then kept and acquired more goods
to furnish our empty future.

Of our memorabilia, your dolls
in forty costumes form the largest
and most eerie species, all
Terri Lees like your earliest partners;
how they seem to gaze and eavesdrop
whenever we duet our good hours and bad,
cozy and uxorious, unlike
the couples in lobby cards I collect—
Citizen Kane, She, Double Indemnity—
who pose all day their dysfunctional
(if eternal) grievances on the walls.

Do these live-in relics make us
more similar or different, as pets
(and babies) make rivals of owners they bond?

My drift is obvious. I'm thinking today,
as if it were an anniversary,
of inward furnishings, the souvenirs
a decades-long acquaintance needs
as it needs jeopardy, trust, humor.
We are each other's enduring matrix,
having co-formed and -possessed ourselves.
No brief union of body parts or
temperaments, no adventure,
no anxiety or gauche memory
that doesn't earn its cherished niche
in the storehouse we share, and grow,
letting what's renewable, my living doll,
make us unbreakable as Bogey and Baby.

Four

Travel is broadening, Father said, so I opened a map.
When I stretched it over the pool table, the shared
desert of Somalia and Ethiopia sundered,
just south of where he'd written, next to Addis Ababa,
"Prester John." Father collected travel books;
as a boy he'd met Richard Halliburton, who told him,
"Seek out the sublime wonders of the world, lad,"
a piece of bad advice he passed along to me.

You'd recognize Father's name, a famous tycoon.
I hide behind a nom de plume, not so
obscure now that I've been profiled in the *Times*
as before my clandestine rendezvous with
Prester John—wait, I'm getting ahead of myself.
"Begin with genesis. That's what Semites do,"
Father said once while probing my secret life.
I said I'd tell him my story if he told me his.

Or rather hers, Mother's, the Great Unmentionable.
"She was . . . not a Semite," he confessed. "In fact,
a blond siren of the genus *Rich man's folly*.
Just returned from the northernmost oil site,
lovesick, I found her in desperate need
of a sizable pension. It's all sordid. She was
the *self*-nurturing kind, unlike your pater.
I gave birth to you, virtually, not she."

He could always sweet-talk me around.
Daddy trotted the globe but discoursed mainly
of petrodollars and pipelines and geopolitics
and what was forbidden women to understand.
"When you become the Wandering Jewess," he said,
"someday you'll meet the One Good Man, the Prester,
and he'll give you not baubles, as I do, but some
birthright, some purpose, some boon of knowledge."

He talked like that. He used words like "tarried,"
"ethereal," "verdure," "profaned," and "behest."
He called himself a "vagabond." In boardrooms
I'm sure he snarled like a Bengal tiger, but to me
he read from *The Royal Road to Romance,* pausing
when his beloved author heightened the diction.
John liked Richard Halliburton too but said
he was "jejune" and lifted his sea-blue eyes to mine.

The twelfth century is my favorite, anyway,
if only for the Leaning Tower of Pisa—if I
were a tall building, I'd be off kilter too.
And it has my favorite poem, *The Rubaiyat,*
my favorite couple, Héloïse and Abelard, and Father's
favorite philosopher, Moses Maimonides.
I wouldn't call Genghis Khan my favorite
barbarian, but he's the kind of lout

Prester John was imagined for, as antidote.
A *dream* of a superpower—not God, exactly,
but if you read his Letter of 1145,
and it's my *favorite* letter of all time, you'll see
how saturated it is with human need,
like those healing waters that close every wound.
It's Shangri-la with salamanders swimming in fire
and shittimwood palaces with jeweled roofs.

Father read me the Letter often. Finally
the bulb switched on: he wants me to *go* there,
Sheba to Solomon, heat-seeking Psyche
aimed at Mr. Perfection with an iron fist.
Never clueless, even before I opened
that winking map, I knew my destination,
some charismatic scouted by Father on *his* trip,
junior Halliburton, to the biblical Cush.

So I outfitted myself for Addis Ababa.
Don't you love the plosives in that name, the nasals
in Abyssinia? Abyssinia—it means "mixed,"
as in the salad of clans and tribes and colors
I marveled at every dust-intensive day.
The language is Amharic. I learned the national anthem:
"March Forward, Dear Mother Ethiopia, Bloom and Flourish."
Gunfire always came with it, like a leitmotif.

I settled into a villa near the Blue Nile,
signing traveler's checks for bentwood chairs,
curtains (or, as Dad would say, silken draperies),
gilded tea sets, tripods with silver feet.
Father sent me some books, including *Prester John*
by John Buchan, useless for my new mission
but fascinating: about a black man who tries
to unite all Africans against the collective baas:

"If they get a leader with prestige enough
to organize a crusade against the white man . . ."—
that sort of stuff, scaring the pants off, well,
me for one. Our ally Haile Selassie
was recently deposed; Nasser was dead,
discredited, but the Ayatollah K.
thundered in the east, and his rain of invective
scorched the Great Rift, if I can mix metaphors.

Nobody called me the Great Satan to my face
or the Whore of Babylon (I dressed discreetly)
or anything but Kind Lady, especially in the bazaars.
Father said ask around for Prester John;
I did and heard plenty about the *sixteenth* century,
when a Somali jihad was snuffed out
by the great king Lebna Dengel, in the marshes
and lunar solitude of the granite peaks.

I figured out that Dengel was a screen,
either for the late Selassie, Ras Tafari,
or his usurper Mengistu, sorcerer and
Soviet pawn, doormat for Cuban troops
and Stasi-variety thugs in ill-fitting uniforms.
"On Eden's walls they splash the Red Terror,"
my servant said, fixing a cup of honey mead
for my aching head at nightfall, sometimes two.

One day a man in white robes came to the door.
"At your service," he said, and more idioms followed:
"heyday," "dumbstruck," "meat loaf," "gut-wrenching"—
obviously American to the core. Yet he spoke
of Ethiopia like a native son, or shrewd
native father, in the manner of their Orthodox Church.
When he took my hand, and once put it to his lips,
I felt a rush of sentiment for his hegemonic cause.

"You are seeking he–who–would–be–Prester John,
Selassie the Second, with an irresistible air force,
a will to power like Ramses or Napoleon,
a wedge for the West against sheikhs and magi,
the possessed and the dispossessed. Someone non-Islam,
skillful in tactics like Lawrence of Arabia,
but Zionist *enough,* not overly zealous,
to back the right horse in Jerusalem.

"Nothing gets done on the Horn without muscle—
here feel this bicep—I can lay out a camel
with a single blow. But it's the *other* power
I cultivate, supraphysical, the flame
of agape guiding us to the source of light. . . .
I have a plan for this leaderless region.
Let me take you out for a bowl of *wat*—
I know a restaurant, alfresco, free of mosquitoes."

Well, he wasn't what I expected, yet
messianic figures don't have a type, do they?
They so often have lower-class beginnings,
a wily charm, seductive really, and speak
their grievances in the argot of the underclass.
"Hyena men," he called the enemy camp.
This rector hated Islam like Charles the Hammer.
Dear pedant, he pounded the table if I nodded off.

John wanted guns, *of course.* Father wired,
"You can't make an omelette, etc.," and all
the time he—John—dressed me for the embassy
and left my card with disgruntled royals
as if I, a *girl,* were a Golda Meir in waiting.
People bowed in the streets, sent gifts of incense,
spoke of Passover with a discernible wink.
Was I so obvious, so unprincipled, a bankroller?

Being Jewish, *as always,* was the problem.
Falasha—black Jews—were a tolerated sect,
maybe the tribe of Benjamin, darkened by the sun
(Ethiopia means "burnt faces"),
but no third force, as foreign to me
as goatherds in the backcountry or sharecroppers
who now labored, poor devils, for the Marxist state.
Powerless—I was a Jewish princess out to sea.

Father did his Pangloss/Imlac best
to cheer me up: "Wear the ritual lion skin
as a glorious emblem of paradise to come."
And added, "I've wired your favorite bank
another hundred grand." "*Dad,* Jews don't
wear lion skin," I wrote back. "The moola
should be deployed against the mullahs, I presume."
"Whatever your little heart desires, precious."

I read Daniel and Exodus and Henry Kissinger.
I plotted, and replotted, the trajectory of Jewish
justice, our potent less-than-one-percent
lashing the global billions forward. All night
I'd sip the pungent, muddy coffee of the highlands
and war game one conditional after another:
if x weapons at New Babylon, or the Temple Mount,
then y apocalypse, victory, and/or terminus.

All holy texts hurried the pace of change,
trumpeting their certainties and glad tidings.
Where I sat, disturbing the peace, in the scented
corner of an ancient wood, nightingales,
for all I knew, waited my passing, and plovers
clung to immemorial trees, still as lichen—
everything so *inanimate,* except petty me
and my walk-on role, laying and lighting the fuse.

I sat by the Nile and wept. The maid fetched John,
who made his pitch again: "My blond treasure,"
he said, "by year's end nothing can resist
the almighty force we shall put into the field.
We will neutralize Egypt, the Sick Man
of North Africa, roll over Sudan, then leap
the Red Sea and play Asian dominoes,
Lionheart with a Star of David under his Cross."

"I love you and so much want to please you,"
I wrote Father, "but this Eric Ambleresque
operative isn't really my cup of tea."
I gave him money for the insurgency, not
much—a mere thousand goes a long way—
but conspiracy's a bottomless pit, isn't it?
Truth is, the more I studied the politics,
the less comfortable I felt as provocateur.

I mean, Ethiopia was a basket case.
King Locust's helpless domain—and a hive
of civil war, its face to the world *never*
a "magnificence that dominates the Three Indies,"
as Prester John wrote from his thirteen-story
tower (with a glass to spy his enemies far off),
more truly UNESCO's starving orphan, a figure
of absolute pathos no warrior would ever redeem.

What bloated stomachs and spindly limbs I saw
when visiting the digs in Hadar, where Lucy's bones
relimned our stunted trees of the human family.
Unwitting ancestor of mine, alpha template
of every hungry child haunting the wasted land.
Closer to Eritrea it got worse: war orphans,
scrounging seeds and drinking at muddy pools,
pulled at my khakis till I gave them bread or coins.

"Seventy-two kings pay tribute to me,"
wrote Prester John. Father had thousands of clients,
greasing the nuts and bolts of his oil-rich
emperies (to use Halliburton's word).
I wanted to make good, to *do* good,
but what power has goodwill against depravity?
Christians had wanted their great priest, John,
to fight the Saracens, and then came Genghis Khan,

who swallowed every non-Mongol on his border,
Gog and Magog, the Great Beast, the Father
of Lies and the Four Horsemen, all in one.
Who told me the world could be improved?
This bauble, this source of amusement (as it was
for travelers of fortune), this charnel house
fit only for cannibals. Genghis Khan beat down
Prester John, the scribes told Marco Polo.

Let's face it, most religious figures are figments.
They show up in only one text (a *big* text, like the Bible).
Maybe Prester John was only a tribal chieftain,
a nomad, a shepherd huffed and puffed
by way of Dame Rumor. One of the Latin kings
of sumptuous Antioch, with an abnormally eloquent
bard under contract, or some bored monk's
fever dream of unlimited imperial power.

I began to box up my new belongings—
my cotton *shammas* and colored scarves,
my ivory chess sets on boards of inlaid ebony—
all the shopping trophies of my tourist life,
but someone alerted John, who showed up with wine.
"Rock bottom is a predictable stage," he soothed.
"Despair, defeatism, par for the course. I too
have sucked up the dregs of this unlucky region.

"'God has commanded my ancestors and myself
to send our people to exterminate the nations'—
excuse me—'the *wicked* nations.' Who said that?
The Khans of Karakorum, the anti-Mohammedans.
Turns out every non-Mongol nation
was on the hordes' hit list and 'bit the dust'
as *our* Homer liked to say. (He too
is proscribed if our side succumbs, as you know.)

"Well, Karakorum is dust. Egypt would be dust
if we choked off the Nile, a strategy I do *not*
recommend. Nobody likes this god-eat-god
scenario less than yours truly. But . . .
there is always a 'but' on this subject . . . deep
in the ideology of this cradle of mankind
it is prophesied a warrior *will* capture Mecca,
join forces with the emperor of Rome,

and drive Islam from the world." He paused for breath.
"Include me out," I said. "This is end-time talking,
the mad stuff of Revelation. OK, I know that power
in a poor country is up for grabs, that 'Prester John'
is a generic title, a buzzword, there for the taking.
But I don't like taking or being taken. And if
you travel into the Nubian desert or the city shops,
you'll find they don't cotton to crusades either."

A dream sorted it out for me. Or tried to.
I stood over the Fountain of Youth, a parrot
perched on my shoulder, chirping the word "John."
I flicked it away and stepped into the pool.
An overwhelming joy possessed me, erotic
and narcissist. I became a child, and Father
called a name from the edge: "Amazon," he said,
and I turned in happy recognition as I woke.

Surely Addis Ababa was not the Land
of Grand Feminie, as the ancients named it,
where women sent arrows into male chests
and necks, yet I felt a thrill of pleasure
after the dream and walked into the murderous
heat, where "the fate of nations"—Father's term—
waited on my whim. It was 1980,
time to draw my wavy line in the Sea of Sand.

Next day I bought a hermitage in Gojam and
filled it with Jewish daughters, most black
and philosophically inclined. I fended off
John, who vowed to take his imperial purposes
elsewhere, even to America, then did just that.
"The Sultan of Egypt still lusts for Jerusalem,"
he warned me in his farewell address, "and someday
when the War at the End of the World buries us

under the 'falling towers' of Mr. Eliot's poem,
you'll turn to me, the protector. Wait and see!"
Fierce John, he was Ethiopia incarnate,
but so was I, in my white robes, like Taitu,
consort of Menelik II, wading into battle.
We learned offset printing in our suites and day
by day produced a series of tracts, or gospels,
now making their way through the Third World.

Phoenix Press launched itself with—what else?—
the Letter of Prester John, fully annotated.
I wrote a skeptical preface, not so much
mocking the wonders, which hardly need debunking,
but tracking the sinkholes of policy, century
by century, as empires giddy at the notion
of a friendly coreligionist in the East
plotted global war and preached Armageddon.

Finally, I got Father's attention. He made a visit.
"You started as the angel of history," he sighed,
"and now you're like the unicorn, horn
embedded in a hardwood tree. In plain view.
Lions will sniff you out, dismember you,
flank by flank." "Not John surely," I said.
"He's busy, at the White House, on the Soviet case.
'One evil empire at a time' is his slogan."

92

"Make light of it," Father said. "The world is unfunny.
Oh, I know his 'puissant monarch' routine
gets tiresome. I too had to stop funding him.
All the cheerfulness went out of it, and where
there had been 'Romance,' as dear Halliburton said,
now there is nothing but truculence. But . . .
if there is no Prester John for us, daughter,
then *we* may be the unicorn. Perhaps we are."

I granted his point. I dropped our plans
to publish Mandeville's travels, that compendium
of nonsense, and let more irony play upon
first one messianic dogma, then its rival.
Partisan groups protested the press in turn:
as we gored their enemies, they forgave
their own wounds. We spread like samizdat,
hand to hand, making no money, winning no prizes.

On the wall, where a crucifix had hung,
we placed a Rastafarian chromo of the emperor,
the Lion of Judah, dressed in the rainbow, his face
radiant as the African sun. Our broadside sheets
of Bob Marley songs are perennial favorites.
Even these joyful tidings we critique,
fearing, like all others, the reggae version of unity:
Black Presbyter but White John writ large.

Oh, it has been a heavenly life! I work
in the composing room all day; after sunset
I walk in the vales, reciting the next day's text.
I compare myself to Menelik, son of Solomon and
Sheba, who converted Ethiopia to Judaism.
I have brought his Talmudic gifts in my caravan,
parsing the false claims and outright ravings
of holy men who conspire against our peace.

We dress like angels, all in white except
those who think of courtship and show indigo
or red. I insist on Innocence as our state,
our hope, our cause, even our crusade.
We are sand in the Juggernaut's gears, modest
though our dress and demeanor, and even our voices
proclaim us . . . pacifist, utopian—
"museful," as my antic father is wont to say.

We Hamitic sisters of the sacramental press
keep the *Book of Marvels* nearby, not the one
with dragons and giants but Halliburton's
guileless tale, when the exotic was unthreatening
and a bright-eyed American boy could wander
like Odysseus through the mysterious world
even to Cambaluc, before sinking, in a storm,
under a Chinese river majestic as the Nile.

ABOUT THE AUTHOR

Laurence Goldstein was born and raised in Los Angeles and received his bachelor's degree from the University of California, Los Angeles, in 1965. After receiving a doctorate from Brown University in 1970, he began a teaching career at the University of Michigan, where he is now a professor of English and, since 1977, the editor of *Michigan Quarterly Review*. He is the author or editor of fourteen books and has published widely in scholarly volumes and literary journals. He lives in Ann Arbor.